"A child's smile is one of life's greatest blessings."

This Book Belongs to...

_____

Joshua and the Four Ducks

Written by Susan DeMil

Illustrated by Helen Foss-Bohm

Susan DeMil
23046 East Main Street
Armada, Michigan 48005
joshuaandthefourducks@gmail.com
www.joshuaandthefourducks.org

Joshua and the Four Ducks

Written by Susan DeMil
©. 2017 All rights reserved.
©. 2017 Artwork by Helen Foss-Bohm

Layout & Design by Dan Waltz
Recorded by Joshua Ackerman

ISBN 13: 978-0-692-84821-0

Library of Congress Control Number: 2017916086

Made in the U.S.A.

Manufactured by Thomson-Shore, Dexter, MI (USA); RMA19LS596, November, 2017

2017 Copyright by Susan DeMil

All rights reserved. No part of this publication may be reproduced, distributed, or transmitted in any form or by any means, including photocopying, recording, or other electronic or mechanical methods, without the prior written permission of the publisher, except in the case of brief quotations embodied in critical reviews and certain other noncommercial uses permitted by copyright law. For permission requests, contact the author.

Susan DeMil
23046 East Main Street
Armada, Michigan 48005
joshuaandthefourducks@gmail.com
www.joshuaandthefourducks.org

Dedication

Through the course of our lives, we meet many people. Occasionally, we come across individuals who are considered exceptional and we are better for having known them. The children at The Rainbow Connection are such people. Their courage, while they are fighting for their lives, is amazing. The enemies who attack these children are not nameless. We know them as Cancer, Hydrocephalus, Leukemia, Hodgkin's Lymphoma and many others too numerous to mention. They attack thousands of children and their families every day. The Rainbow Connection allows these children and their families to make beautiful memories together and to forget about their pain and sorrow for a short time.

All profits of this book will benefit The Rainbow Connection which makes dreams come true for Michigan children with life threatening illnesses and provides emergency support services to the family. Support services include information, referral, special summer and holiday get-togethers and, perhaps most important of all, a listening ear to families battling a child's life threatening illness.

Please tell your friends and family about our story, so 'together' we can continue to help these brave children.

The Rainbow Connection
Making dreams come true for Michigan children with life threatening illnesses

621 West University • Rochester, MI 48307
248.601.9474
www.rainbowconnection.org

It was a beautiful, crystal clear, blue-sky day in Michigan. Riding down the dirt road in our station wagon, Joshua peered out the window. He noticed the farms we passed had all kinds of animals in their yards. Joshua wondered about the animals and asked, "How come we don't have any dogs or cats?"

"Well," I began, "your Daddy doesn't want to have one."

"Well, how come?" Joshua questioned. He was a curious little boy who always wanted to figure things out. Being three was a big deal and learning new things was on top of his list.

All of a sudden, I saw a sign that read, "Ducks for Sale." I decided it would be fun to stop and see the ducks, so we pulled into the drive. Joshua jumped out of the car as soon as I opened his door. He ran towards the pen, with the ducks. Joshua giggled with laughter as he watched all the little ducklings run about making little peep-like noises.

"Can we get some, please?" asked Joshua.

I replied, "Why not!," and told the farmer we would like to buy some of his ducklings.

"Well," the farmer said. "How many would you like?"

Joshua yelled out, "FOUR, 'cause I am going to be four next!"

"Sold," the farmer said. He gave Joshua a box, and to his delight Joshua was told to pick out the ones he would like.

It was a big job as the little ducklings were darting all about here and there. However, my little Joshua was determined and he shortly caught all four ducklings!

As we headed back home, Joshua held onto his box of little ducks. He was glad the farmer had given him a bag of food to go with them. He couldn't wait to get home and show his friends and his Daddy his new pets. I thought, we have a new adventure and hoped Daddy would like the ducks, as well.

When came home and decided to put the ducklings in the bathtub. They were paddling their little feet and were just so sweet, when all of a sudden the littlest one started to sink. I quickly picked it up and wrapped it in a washcloth. Joshua started to cry.

"There now, don't cry," I said.

"Will it be ok?" Joshua asked.

I said "Let's call Grandma and Grandpa Demick. They grew up on a farm and they will know exactly what to do."

So we called them. We told Grandma what happened and she said to get the baby duckling under a light where he can warm up. Rub him softly with a towel to help him get dry. Grandma explained that the mother duck often rubs oil from her own oil gland near the base of her tail, called the uropygial gland, often nicknamed the preening gland. She rubs her bill on her preening gland almost immediately after the ducklings are hatched. She puts the oil on the babies which helps coat the down feathers with that oil, so they won't sink like your duckling did. That oil helps waterproof the down feathers. As soon as their feathers come in, about six to eight weeks after they are born, they will be able to preen themselves and they will swim just fine. She suggested that the next time you put them in the water, just put in a little bit. We sent our love to them and we were glad Daddy's parents had grown up on a farm.

Just then, Daddy walked in and looked down at the bathtub and asked, "What do we have here?"

Joshua popped up like toast from a toaster and said, "I have four ducks!"

Daddy looked at me and I said, "Well you said no dogs or cats, so we bought ducks!"

He laughed and said, "Well, you got me there."

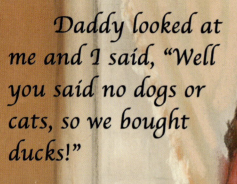

"Can we keep them?" asked Joshua.

Daddy said "Okay, but you'll have to take care of them," he answered.

Jashua said, "I will!"

As the weeks went by, we watched the ducks grow. All the kids in the neighborhood stopped by every day for a visit. We had a little blue pool for them to play in, and everyone had so much fun.

Then one day Uncle Steve came by for a visit. He said, "I have an idea for your ducks." He went to his truck and brought out some chicken wire and some wooden stakes. He said, "Joshua, you come here and help me. You see, you five on a lake and ducks love water, so we will build an enclosure."

Joshua frowned and asked, "What is an enclosure?"

"I will show you." Uncle Steve said.

As the boys got to work on their project I went inside and made some chocolate chip cookies.

When I came out, I was surprised. There in the lake was the chicken wire attached to the wooden stakes, in a circle. Our happy ducks were swimming about.

"Well done, boys!"

We sat on the edge of the lake with our feet in the water. We ate our cookies and drank our milk. I thought, what a splendid day it was, indeed!

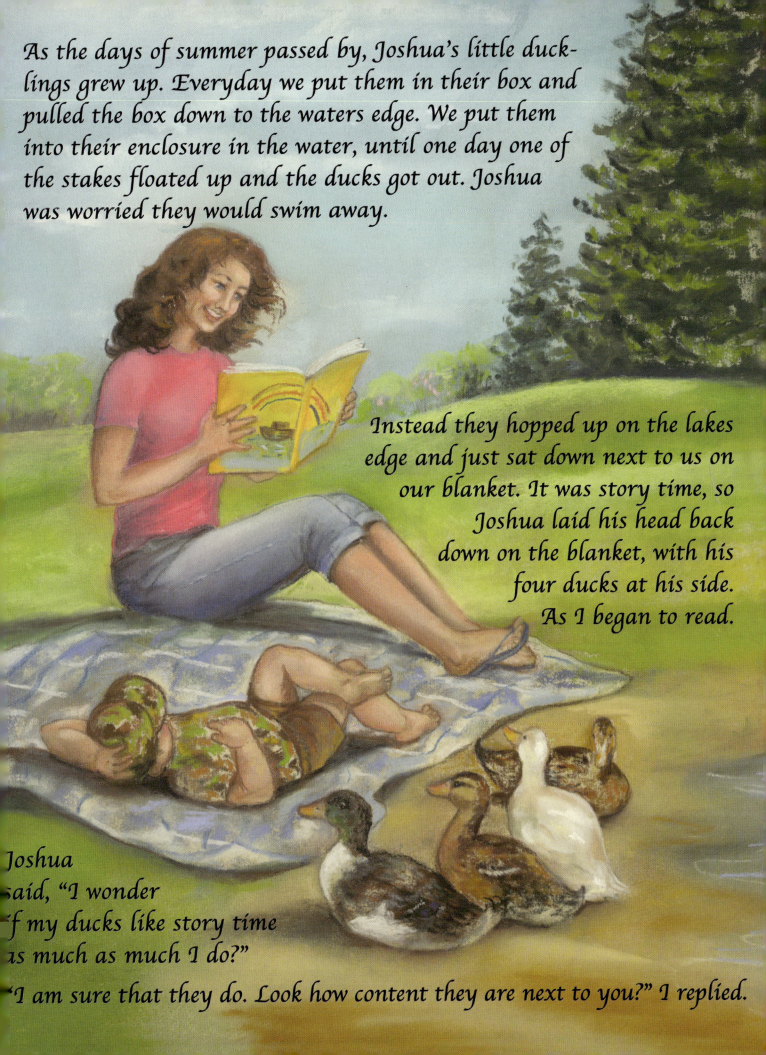

As the days of summer passed by, Joshua's little ducklings grew up. Everyday we put them in their box and pulled the box down to the waters edge. We put them into their enclosure in the water, until one day one of the stakes floated up and the ducks got out. Joshua was worried they would swim away.

Instead they hopped up on the lakes edge and just sat down next to us on our blanket. It was story time, so Joshua laid his head back down on the blanket, with his four ducks at his side. As I began to read.

Joshua said, "I wonder if my ducks like story time as much as much I do?"

"I am sure that they do. Look how content they are next to you?" I replied.

When we were done with the story, we always went for a walk around the lake. We started out that day and Joshua's ducks followed us, one by one. The children in the neighborhood would often go with us as well. We sang songs every time as we walked.

One of Joshua's favorite songs was the "Army Song." We all sang, We are in the army now. Nothing can stop us now. Sound off, 1-2, sound off 3-4, come on down 1,2,3,4! The ducks would quack, the children would laugh. Joshua would always say, "You know I am going to be in the Army someday."

I said "I know you will, darling."

As fall was coming to an end one morning, I saw our dear ducks fly away. They knew it was time to fly south for the winter. Joshua wanted to know why they had to leave. I told him they are off on an adventure, just like you will do someday. It was the process of life.

Joshua said, "I am not ready to go."

I said, "It's not your time yet, but just like your ducks, you will know 'inside' when it is your time to move on in your adventures in life. Just know that we will enjoy every step in our lives."

Winter passed and we often thought about our ducks. When the weather started to warm up one spring morning, we heard a familiar sound. Quack, quack, quack! Joshua ran to the door, opened it, and there were his ducks! He laughed so hard and said, "They are back and they are hungry." He ran for the kitchen and grabbed some bread. He then ran to his room and grabbed one of his favorite books, a story about Noah's Ark. He looked out the door, then counted them, "1,2,3,4, they are all here," Joshua said. "Four and now I am four!" He ran for his room and grabbed a book. He looked at me and said, "Come on; they haven't had a story all winter. I bet they are really ready for one now."

We grabbed our blanket and sat down by the water's shore. The ducks waddled right after us. Joshua and I sat down, the ducks sat next to us. I started to read and looked down at Joshua.

He had the biggest smile on his face. I thought, what a happy surprise for my big four year old. This would be my favorite part of the day.

We had many summers on the lake and each year our ducks would fly back. The children in the neighborhood called me the duck lady. And as Joshua grew up and he did go into the Army. He flew in the air, jumped out of planes with his parachute, and went on many adventures in his life, just like his ducks!

Fun Facts about Duck's

1. Feather- One of the light, soft fluffy parts that cover the underside of the duck called down feathers and then on top the larger contour feathers. There are so many on the underside of their bodies, ducks can swim in the coldest water and remain comfortable.

2. Webbed-Having folded skin or tissue between an animal's toes or fingers; webbed feet help ducks swim better.

3. Preen-To clean and arrange feathers with a beak; ducks spread oil from their Uropygial gland, nicknamed preening gland all over their feathers to help them float. The oil prevents the water from absorbing into the feathers.

4. Baby ducks will sink in water if the Mother duck does not oil the fluffy, water-absorbing down with oils from her own gland near the base of her tail. She does this preening on the babies as soon as they hatch! Within four to six weeks old the baby ducklings will start getting their feathers and are well adjusted to preening themselves. By eight weeks old the ducklings will be fully feathered.

5. Waddle-To walk with short steps while moving from side to side.

6. Bill-Duck bills are the ducks nose and mouth of the duck. Long and well adapted for collecting food from water, catching flying insects and rooting out underground bugs. With nostrils located near the head on the top of bill, ducks can dabble in shallow water and breathe at the same time.

7. Feeding-Ducks diet is 90 percent vegetable mater, seeds, berries, fruit, nuts, bulbs, and grasses. Our ducks liked grapes! Ten percent is animal matter such as insects, mosquito larvae, snails, slugs, leeches, worms, small fish and even a tadpole. Sand and gravel are picked up while they are eating and actually helps as grinding stones in the gizzard. Ducks feed by dabbling and tipping up in shallow water, while drilling in mud and foraging on land. Baby ducks need their meal mixed with water.

8. Eyes-The vision of ducks are very sharp because of their location, ducks can see nearly 360 degrees without moving their heads. This makes it possible for a feeding duck to keep a good lookout for danger.

9. Behavior-Ducks have gentle behavior, they are rather shy. Just like you and I each duck is a little different. They like patterns and doing the same things and can adapt to their surroundings. Our ducks liked going on our walks every day.

10. Space and Shelter-Ducklings grow fast, they soon out grow their box within a few weeks. They become large, active and messy. They need a clean, dry, warm enclosure for good health. They need to be protected against weather and predatory animals.

Where it all began...

Circa 1978 - 1983

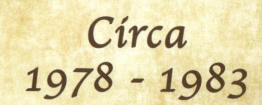

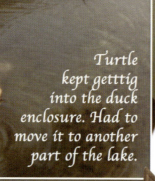

Turtle kept getttig into the duck enclosure. Had to move it to another part of the lake.

Joshua was happy to see his ducks after the long winter!

Ducks are getting big!

Grandpa & Grandma Demick with little Joshua!

Grandma Demick loved fishing with her Grandson!

I am very excited to share with you, this true story about Joshua and our Four Duck's.

One of my granddaughter's Rory Ann, would always ask me to tell her about this story. One day she said, "Grandmama, you should write a book about Uncle Josh's ducks, then other children can read about them." A few years later, while flying to Florida, I was trying to think of another way to raise more money for the sick children at Rainbow Connection. My husband and I always played backgammon when flying. All of a sudden he said, would you mind if I slept a little bit? I said, sure. Now that was odd, as in over 18 years of flying together he never slept. I closed my eyes, prayed and then I thought about the book. Now every good real estate broker always has paper at hand. I then put pen to paper and began to write.

After our vacation, I contacted a good friend, Helen Foss-Bohm, and asked her if she would consider being the illustrator for the book. She said, "Susan you won't believe this today while at an Art Show, I had been approached by three different individuals, they came up to me independently, telling me I should be an illustrator for a children's book." No one ever said that to her before. It was as if God was giving us his blessing. Every step of the way, we have been guided to find caring people to help with this project, Dana Lehman, Dan Waltz and Joshua Ackerman.

I have enjoyed working with Rainbow Connection for the last 16 years. Ingrid Todt, Barb Massie and Brenda Moore are real angels on earth helping these children! With the help of many of my friends and family, especially my dear friend Betty Hunt. We have been able to help grant wishes to 82 children with our "Wishes Can Come True", golf outings and collection buckets. My hope is that anyone who reads this will be inspired to do something to help these beautiful children.

I want to thank my son Joshua for his wonderful spirit in life. His dedication in serving our country. Also, giving his blessing with this book to help the children. My husband Robert DeMil for his support and understanding my commitment through the years. My Dad, Gary F. Gabler for encouraging me that I can achieve my goals. Our six children Joshua, Jaclyn, Tammy, Katie, Andre, Amanda.

Our fifteen Grandchildren, Cody, Amaya, Alyssa, Hunter, Victoria, Katrina, Gianluca, Rory Ann, Jax, Alexander, Evan, Charlie, Teagn Rylee, Logan, Liam.

It has been a beautiful journey and I have learned a lot through the years meeting the parents and children who have been so ill and yet only are worried about their loved ones. It is humbling at best and I admire their courage. My grandfather, Clyde W. Gabler once told me, Susan Ann, "Every day is a challenge and we must face our challenges. More importantly every day is precious, use each day wisely. No matter what comes your way, the experience's you have, will one day enable you to help someone else who is not as strong as you! He sure was right!

Helen Foss-Bohm has been drawing since she was a five year old child. She recollects the times when her Mother came home from the market with her meat purchases wrapped in the traditional, heavy, white wrapping. Helen would gather the paper and use it to draw on, it served as a wonderful medium for her sketches!

When Helen was seven years old, her teacher in school would encourage Helen to draw pictures on the long, tall, chalk boards that covered the wall. She drew kids skating, seasonal scenes and animals to her classmates delight. When Helen was nine years old, her teacher encouraged her to pursue her interest in art by introducing her to the Detroit Institute of Arts. During their trip, Helen observed a woman in the Kresge storefront window drawing on an easel. Helen said to her teacher, "I would love to do that someday." Her teacher assured Helen she would indeed!

Helen is blessed with a God-given artistic talent, and she has passed that same creative flair and gift to her children. Over the years, Helen has utilized her painting talent to enhance local historic buildings, schools and business. She is a skilled and proficient calligraphist, both in pen and brush. Helen is an active participant in pastel drawing groups and has published several art pieces in the past 20 years. Her colorful pastels can be found displayed in her church, private homes, and in an occasional local boutique.

Helen and her husband, Charlie, are happy together sharing a farmer's life on an 80 acre registered Holstein farm in Michigan. They enjoy their involvement with their extended families lives, which includes six married children, twelve grandchildren and two great grandchildren!

Helen was truly delighted to be the illustrator of "Joshua and the Four Ducks", and with the knowledge that it would forever help wishes come true to the sick children at Rainbow Connection, the decision was an easy one to make!

The Rainbow Connection

When a child is allowed to dream, it is pure magic! They are able to focus on something good and positive, giving them hope and lifting their spirits. It is the rainbow in the midst of a family's storm.

The Rainbow Connection isn't just about a dream of going somewhere or doing something special, it is about the child being allowed to dream - to be a kid. It's about the *family* reuniting around something other than hospital visits, medicine and doctors.

A dream come true strengthens a family and creates memories that will be cherished *forever*.

"Granting wishes is a very simple way of saying that you give sick kids and their families the opportunity to share joy, make memories, and forget about the struggle, even if for a moment. Sam's granted wish gave him and our family freedom to dream, permission to pause, and hopeful anticipation of good things to come."

-Gina, Sam's Mom

More than a *Wish*

The *Special Response* program refers Rainbow Connection Families experiencing hardships to human service or consumer agencies and when necessary, offers financial assistance.

The *Enhancement* program continues to link arms with Rainbow Connection children and their families through respite activities.

Scholarships are awarded to select Rainbow Connection children who continue education beyond high school.

The Rainbow Connection
621 W. University • Rochester, MI 48307
248.601.9474 • RainbowConnection.org

Ways to *Help*

Personal Gifts

Donate
Donations of all sizes make a difference. To donate visit rainbowconnection.org

Honor A Loved One
The Pathway of Angels is a brick pathway winding through The Rainbow Connection garden. Whether streamed in sunlight or dusted with gently falling snow, our pathway offers a serene setting for reflection.

With a donation of $100 your customized engraved brick will become part of the magic of The Rainbow Connection.

You Shop. They Give.

Amazon Smile
AmazonSmile is a website operated by Amazon with the same products, prices, and shopping features as Amazon.com. The difference is that when you shop on AmazonSmile, the AmazonSmile Foundation will donate 0.5% of eligible purchases to your charity of choice. To select The Rainbow Connection, simply set up a profile at **smile.amazon.com** and select The Rainbow Connection as your charity of choice.

Kroger Community Rewards
If you shop at Kroger and have a Plus Card you can help The Rainbow Connection! Select The Rainbow Connection as your charitable organization at **kroger.com/account/enrollCommunityRewardsNow**. Then every time you shop and swipe your Plus Card, Kroger will make a contribution to The Rainbow Connection!

Get Your Employer Involved

Casual Days
Ask your employer to hold a "Casual Day" fundraiser - employees donate to dress casual on a designated day. Already have a Casual Day? Suggest a company pot luck, bake sale or BBQ to benefit The Rainbow Connection.

Matching Funds
Ask your Personnel or Human Resource Department if your company participates in a Matching Fund Program and how you can participate.

Corporate Sponsorship
Sponsoring one of our major events provides an opportunity for companies to showcase their support in a highly visible way while making dreams come true for Michigan children.